ENGLISH LANGUAGE: PAPER ONE

An AQA Study Guide

ANTHONY WALKER-COOK

First published in 2021 by Accolade Tuition Ltd
71-75 Shelton Street
Covent Garden
London WC2H 9JQ
www.accoladetuition.com
info@accoladetuition.com

ISBN 978-1-913988-06-7

FIRST EDITION
1 3 5 7 9 10 8 6 4 2

Contents

Editor's Foreword

If you're enrolled on AQA's English Language GCSE, you will be taking on two separate papers: Paper One – which deals with fiction – and Paper Two – which deals with non-fiction. This book (as you might have guessed from its title!) is designed to guide you specifically through Paper One.

Now, before anything else, it's important to briefly outline what Paper One looks like. The paper is comprised of two sections. The first section looks fairly similar to comprehension papers students will have been doing throughout secondary school: you will be given an extract from a piece of fiction (it'll be from the past 120 years or so), and you will face four questions that deal with this extract. These four questions – while of course tailored to the extract in question – *always* take the same format, and are *always* worth a total of 40 marks (4 marks for the first question; 8 marks for the second and third; and 20 marks for the fourth).

The medieval poet, Geoffrey Chaucer, is sometimes referred to as the 'Father of the English Language.' Above: the Chaucerian equivalent of a selfie.

Then, once you've cleared that hurdle, you'll have the second section to contend with – the creative writing section. And you'll have a choice between two options: one that asks you to write a story, and one that asks you to write a description. This task – whichever of the two you choose – is worth a further 40 marks.

I fully appreciate that this may all sound complex and daunting, but don't despair – as you work through this guide, the very talented Anthony (the author!) will take you through things step-by-step and shine a light into Paper One's every nook and cranny.

And yet, having said all that, it is important to emphasise that this guide is *not* merely designed to familiarise you with Paper One's structure; after all, there are already other great guides out there that do just that. Rather, this guide – by proffering model answers, dissecting this exemplar material, and painstakingly delving into AQA's mark-schemes – will seek to demonstrate *how* to ensure you are covering all bases and picking up every available mark. For while it is true that the extract is unseen and thus you can never prepare fully in advance, there are all sorts of tactics and techniques that you can memorise and master before you set foot in that exam hall. In fact, it's precisely because we felt that no other guide adequately grapples with these techniques – adequately spells out how best to approach the paper's assorted challenges – that we decided to put together this dedicated technique guide for this exam in the first place!

They've been doing GCSE exams for a while now!

In short, our hope is that this book, by demonstrating *how* to tackle Paper One's challenges, will help you feel more confident in doing so yourself. I believe that it is also worth mentioning that for most of the questions you'll encounter in Paper One (in fact *all* except for Question 1) there is no one answer the examiner is looking for. That is, while Anthony's work may represent "model" material, someone else's answers could be quite different and yet be just as effective at nabbing the marks (this is especially true of the creative writing task in the paper's latter half!). I won't pretend your exam is likely to be *fun* – my memory of the exams is pretty much the exact opposite. But still, this is one of the very few chances that you will get at GCSE level to actually be creative. And to my mind at least, that was always more enjoyable – if *enjoyable* is the right word – than simply demonstrating that I had memorised loads of facts.

R. P. Davis, 2021

Note on Structure

Presented in this guide are four worked exams. In the first set of responses, I discuss the Assessment Objectives and consolidate your knowledge of what is expected for each question. In the second set, I outline my tips and tricks for each style of question. In the third set I suggest why some students struggle in their answers to the questions based on Examiner's Reports. Finally, the fourth set just presents model answers with no introduction or commentary – they are for you to annotate and to explore the ways in which all of the questions for this exam can be answered.

Sample Paper One

SECTION A: F. SCOTT FITZGERALD'S THE GREAT GATSBY; SECTION B: A SPECIAL EVENT

F. Scott Fitzgerald's The Great Gatsby

SECTION A: READING

Source A: This extract is from the beginning of Chapter 3 of F. Scott Fitzgerald's *The Great Gatsby*. The story depicts fashionable society of 1920s America.

1   There was music from my neighbour's house through the summer nights. In his blue gardens men and girls came and went like moths among the whisperings and the champagne and the stars. At high tide in the afternoon I watched his guests diving from the tower of his raft, or taking the sun on the hot sand of his beach while his
5   two motor-boats slit the waters of the Sound, drawing aquaplanes over cataracts of foam. On week-ends his Rolls-Royce became an omnibus, bearing parties to and from the city between nine in the morning and long past midnight, while his station wagon scampered like a brisk yellow bug to meet all trains. And on Mondays eight servants, including an extra gardener, toiled all day with mops and scrubbing-brushes
10   and hammers and garden-shears, repairing the ravages of the night before.

Every Friday five crates of oranges and lemons arrived from a fruiterer in New York – every Monday these same oranges and lemons left his back door in a pyramid of pulpless halves. There was a machine in the kitchen which could extract the juice of two hundred oranges in half an hour if a little button was pressed two hundred times
15   by a butler's thumb.

At least once a fortnight a corps of caterers came down with several hundred feet of canvas and enough colored lights to make a Christmas tree of Gatsby's enormous garden. On buffet tables, garnished with glistening hors-d'oeuvre, spiced baked hams

20 crowded against salads of harlequin designs and pastry pigs and turkeys bewitched to a dark gold. In the main hall a bar with real brass rail was set up, and stocked with gins and liquors and with cordials so long forgotten that most of his female guests were too young to know one from another.

By seven o-clock the orchestra has arrived, no thin five-piece affair, but a whole pitful of oboes and trombones and saxophones and viols and cornets and piccolos, and low
25 and high drums. The last swimmers have come in from the beach now and are dressing up-stairs; the cars from New York are parked five deep in the drive, and already the halls and salons and verandas are gaudy with primary colors, and hair bobbed in strange new ways, and shawls beyond the dreams of Castile. The bar is in full swing, and floating rounds of cocktails permeate the garden outside, until the air
30 is alive with chatter and laughter, and casual innuendo and introductions forgotten on the spot, and enthusiastic meetings between women who never knew each other's names.

The lights grow brighter as the earth lurches away from the sun, and now the orchestra is playing yellow cocktail music, and the opera of voices pitches a key
35 higher. Laughter is easier minute by minute, spilled with prodigality, tipped out at a cheerful word. The groups change more swiftly, swell with new arrivals, dissolve and form in the same breath; already there are wanderers, confident girls who weave here and there among the stouter and more stable, become for a sharp, joyous moment the centre of a group, and then, excited with triumph, glide on through the sea-change
40 of faces and voices and color under the constantly changing light.

Question One: Guidance

Question One assesses AO1, which is about reading comprehension. Having read the text you've got to synthesise (meaning, combining a variety of information) this for your own uses. You might also have to make inferences, which is drawing a conclusion from the text based on evidence.

Before you even begin to think about answering any questions, take time to read the source. Carefully annotate the work and use the opening few minutes to settle your nerves. Focus first on comprehension and then lightly annotate the source with any of your initial impressions. It'll help you feel in control of the material.

Question One: Exemplar

Read again the first part of the source, from **lines 1 to 6.**

List **four** things about Gatsby's guests from this part of the source.

[4 marks]

1. *They party throughout the summer.*
2. *Lots of guests come and go.*
3. *They drink champagne.*
4. *During the day they go swimming.*

Question Two: Guidance

Question Two invites the student to continue working through the extract, covering perhaps six to ten lines, and it wants you to analyse how a writer uses language to **describe** something. You should spend 10 minutes on this question.

Questions Two and Three are assessed with Assessment Objective Two (AO2), which asks you to 'explain, comment on and analyse' the use of language and structure. These three skills need careful definition and they do work in a hierarchy (by that, I mean "explain" is the lowest skill whereas "analyse" is the highest, with comment in the middle).

Explaining how a writer uses language means to describe, paraphrase or write about the passage in general terms. At this level, students show they understand the text, but offer little by way of focusing on effect.

When a student is **commenting on** the text, they are showing that they can explore the writer's methods to produce an effect, but it does not fully engage with the text enough to be called analysis.

Analysis means to break down the passage into the techniques or choices made by an author and to then write about the effect of these choices in your work. In doing so, you'll be synthesising the material (that is, understanding and then using it to make a point).

You will be provided with some bullet points to help stimulate your ideas. Some students use these points as a way of structuring their response, but it is worth stressing here that there is no requirement for you to cover all aspects of these points. Often, in fact, it is the students who are narrow in their focus, yet who explore the text in detail, that do the best.

Also, on an issue of practicality – the exam board will provide the extract for Question Two in a box above the question. Before beginning Question Two, make sure you re-read the text and annotate it: keep the text as fresh in your mind as possible!

Question Two: Exemplar

Look in detail at this extract, from lines 6 to 15 of the source:

On week-ends his Rolls-Royce became an omnibus, bearing parties to and from the city between nine in the morning and long past midnight, while his station wagon scampered like a brisk yellow bug to meet all trains. And on Mondays eight servants, including an extra gardener, toiled all day with mops and scrubbing-brushes and hammers and garden-shears, repairing the ravages of the night before.

Every Friday five crates of oranges and lemons arrived from a fruiterer in New York – every Monday these same oranges and lemons left his back door in a pyramid of pulpless halves. There was a machine in the kitchen which could extract the juice of two hundred oranges in half an hour if a little button was pressed two hundred times by a butler's thumb.

How does the writer use language here to describe the preparations for the party?

You could include the writer's choice of:

- Words and phrases
- Language features and techniques
- Sentence forms.

[8 marks]

From the beginning of the extract, [1] *Fitzgerald emphasises the large-scale organisation needed to prepare for the party. Gatsby's Rolls-Royce, a car that signifies class and wealth, becomes an 'omnibus', used to shepherd people throughout the day,* ***perhaps reducing its prestige or emphasising his wealth.*** [2] *Meanwhile the simile that describes how the station wagon 'scampered like a brisk yellow bug' stresses how fast the vehicle has to move to collect the ever-growing number of guests from the train station.*

This is then matched by the point that ***'eight servants, including an extra gardener' work*** [3] *all day to repair the damage done before. Not only does beginning the sentence with*

*1) **It can be best to methodically work through the extract (that way, you're covering it in detail). This also sets up themes that can be explored throughout your answer.** 2) **I've provided two interpretations here to show a perceptive understanding of language.***

'And' imply the long list of jobs that need doing before each evening's events but also in using **'ravages'** to describe the repair work needed Fitzgerald suggests the violent damage these parties do to Gatsby's property.

3) ***Notice throughout this answer (and the rest) how my quotations are integrated into my prose.*** *4)* ***This listing language can be a good way to give the impression that you are ranging throughout the text.*** *5)* ***It's fine to refer specifically to certain lines in the source for clarity.*** *6)* ***Just a neat concluding sentence to tie everything together and answer the question.***

Furthermore,[4] *Fitzgerald focuses on the 'crates of oranges and lemons' that arrive to be juiced, the sheer mass of which is emphasised through the repetition of the same line in* **line 12**.[5] *By Monday, these fruits leave 'in a pyramid of pulpless halves', with Fitzgerald's metaphor showing how these parties achieve a grandeur of something akin to the ancient Egyptians. The metaphor also suggests, then, that these parties have an almost mythical status. But Fitzgerald also describes the mundane activity that provides such a pile of fruit: a servant pushes a button for each piece of fruit to be squashed, with the repetition of 'two hundred' within the same sentence stressing the repetitive nature of the work.* **Therefore, though these parties are lavish, Fitzgerald's language actually stresses the hard work needed to prepare for them.**[6]

Question Three: Guidance

Though students are often confused about Question Three – in 2018 many did not achieve more than 4 marks out of the maximum 8 – the *skill set* required is the exact same as Question Two: that is, your whole answer should be filled with analysis (or, AO2). Meaning, you need to offer specific comments on the effect of the structural features used by the author.

Everything I've outlined above on Question Two regarding writing on effect also applies for Question Three. It has been noted that students who do better in Question Three tend not to overcomplicate it with subject terminology but are receptive to simpler changes. Why, for example, has a writer used a short sentence? For effect? For emphasis? To capture an emotion? Perhaps, it all depends on the context of the passage. But whenever you read a text, be alert to how it is structured – does it have short or long sentences, or extended paragraphs or brief ones – and think about how that influences the content. If you can think in this way, then you're analysing structure.

Aim to spend around 10 minutes on this question, just like Question Two.

Question Three: Exemplar

You now need to think about the **whole** of the source.

This text is from the beginning of a chapter.

How has the writer structured the text to interest you as a reader?

You could write about:

- What the writer focuses your attention on at the beginning of the source.
- How and why the writer changes this focus as the source develops
- Any other structural features that interest you.

[8 marks]

Fitzgerald uses structure to interest the reader by accretively* adding points to the description of the party and its preparations. **The opening of the source**[1] *is broad and generic but by the end of the extract it is clear that more than just 'music' was to be found at Gatsby's house.*

There is an attention to detail that draws the narrator in only for them to be distracted by something else: for example, **the third paragraph begins** *by noting the lights in Gatsby's 'enormous garden'* **before moving onto** *the buffet tables laden with food* **and then onto**[2] *the intoxicating bar in the main hall. This quick change of focus is also aided by Fitzgerald's sentences, which are often long and sprawling and demonstrate the narrator's (and our own) fascination with this luxurious world.*

Fitzgerald also **uses repetition**[3] *to stress how the orchestra was 'no thin five-piece affair', describing 'a whole pitful of oboes and trombones and saxophones and viols and coronets and piccolos, and low and high drums.' The writer uses 'and' to add instruments to the group, slowly building it up and overall focusing on its size.*

By the final paragraph, *the intoxicating party is in full swing, the focus shifting across the faceless attendees. In contrast to the long sentences earlier that described the preparations for the party, here* **Fitzgerald litters his sentences with commas**,[4] *creating short, pithy statements that capture the experiences ('groups change more swiftly, swell with new arrivals, dissolve and form in the same breath') of each attendee.* **By the**

1) Again, begin your answer with the beginning of the source, but noticing how the source has changed by the end means you will be gaining marks from the very beginning. 2) Here I'm ranging across the third paragraph and not getting too focused on details. Instead I'm showing how Fitzgerald zooms in and out of the text, and the effect this has – I've combined this with an analysis of his sentence structures to demonstrate I understand the various ways in which structure can be assessed. 3) Another technique is discussed here, as always, with a focus on its effect at the end. 4) In my final paragraph I'm showing how the text changes and analysing structure at the level of sentence organisation, again showing a strong awareness of how a writer uses structure.

5) I return to the reader at the end just to make sure it is clear to the examiner that I am answering the question.

end of the source, then, readers are also experiencing the 'constantly changing light' described by the author.[5]

* If something is 'accretive', it means it is gradually growing or increasing. Be aware of how lists accretively add to the overall tone of the passage.

Question Four: Guidance

This is the final question for Section A, and the first thing you should note is that it is worth 20 marks – so it's worth 25% of the entire Paper – therefore it is meant to be challenging and it is important that you get your timings right during the exam so that you have enough time to spend on this answer. You need to spend at least 20 minutes on this question.

This question is asking you to evaluate both the ideas in the source and the methods. AO4 is about evaluation: so, you need to assess to what extent the writer achieves the purpose and message implicit in the work. Don't worry, we haven't missed AO3: that assessment objective is examined only in Paper Two.

Question Four also requires you to use textual references: again, this means short and useful quotations that aid your point. Referring to the text in detail also counts towards this.

The exam board have noted how having a 'methods-based' approach can improve answers. All the skills you have practiced before – analysis of language and structure – can be used again here (though the analytical points you made in Question Three should not really be repeated) but now it is about **the success** of the effect of these features on the reader.

It is important, therefore, that you build in evaluative language into your response, with words and phrases such as: 'successfully', 'powerfully', 'clever use of', 'this is effective because...', 'the writer's creative use of...', 'innovative', 'inventive'.

You want to be using this language from the opening line of your response.

Question Four: Exemplar

Focus this part of your answer on the second part of the source, from **line 20 to the end**.

Upon reading this extract, a student said, 'It is hard to know whether or not the narrator is attracted to or disgusted by the party.'

To what extent do you agree?

In your response, you could:

- Evaluate how the writer depicts the party.
- Consider how the guests are portrayed.
- Support your response with references to the text.

[20 marks]

*1) **I am using the terms of the question so the examiner knows I am answering the question from the beginning.** 2) **I am using brackets to quote from the text just to support my point in a way that is unobtrusive to my writing.** 3) **I am linking back to the question at the end of the paragraph.** 4) **Notice I am always using the writer's name throughout every one of my answers – this is a subtle way of showing you know that writing is an active process.** 5) **Another brief detail to demonstrate that I am ranging throughout the text.***

*From the beginning of the extract, Fitzgerald **carefully balances tones of attraction and disgust, leaving the reader unsure exactly of how the narrator is responding to the party.**[1] This tonal effect is achieved often through unsure word choices or occasional phrases that complicate the description of the party. For example, the bar in the main hall has drinks 'so long forgotten that most of his female guests were too young to know one from another.' Whilst there is a mystical quality to these drinks, they are also redundant and inaccessible to these young women. This ambivalence continues into the description of the house, which has rooms and verandas that 'are gaudy with primary colors'. Given the sentence goes on to describe the hair styles of the party-goers **('bobbed in new ways'),**[2] it could be suggested that the 'gaudy' primary colours refers to the clothing worn by the guests. Also the detail that cars are 'parked five deep in the drive' not only shows how many people are at the party but also how busy and full the house must be. This tone of excess continues throughout the extract, **making it difficult to define how the narrator feels about the party.**[3]*

*Once the extract shifts into the events of the party, this tone of tired wonder continues. There are 'floating rounds of cocktails' moving around the space, suggesting a magical power behind them. But, the narrator is also unable to focus: through a long sentence connected by the repetition of 'and', **Fitzgerald shifts**[4] from the drinks to the 'casual innuendo and introductions' that are being shared to the 'enthusiastic meetings between women'. Small details also suggest these people are all vapid: **the introductions are 'forgotten on the spot'.**[5]*

For all the lustre of the event, then, Fitzgerald continues to cleverly provide hints throughout that all is not as glamorous as it seems.

The final paragraph of the extract begins by describing the setting sun, but Fitzgerald uses this moment to emphasise the amount of alcohol consumed during the party: the earth 'lurches away from the sun', as if the earth itself is drunk, **with 'lurches' imbuing the lines with suggestions of a lack of control and again complicating the reader's impression of the party.**[6] The party increasingly becomes overwhelming, with conversation described as an 'opera of voices' that moves 'a key higher'; Fitzgerald's metaphor juxtaposes the traditional concept of the opera as a higher form of singing with its actual presence here from the conversations of the guests. Amidst this cacophony, the groups of guests are said to 'swell', which implies a pregnancy to the party that threatens to burst. There is thus a tension in the air that makes reading the extract almost uncomfortable.

*6) **This is the sort of analysis you would expect in Question Two – here, however, I have tied the point back to the question.** 7) **And this is the sort of analysis you would expect in Question Three – it is all the same skills, just with a different focus.** 8) **I am re-iterating the terms of the question in my closing sentence just to signal to the examiner that my response has been focused.** 9) **I have concluded with some quotes from the text as a point of style and to avoid repeating myself.***

But then, **in the final part of the extract, Fitzgerald shifts focus**[7] to some girls 'who weave here and there among the stouter and more stable' guests. The use of the word 'weave' adds a delicacy to their movement, which matches with the later verb 'glide' that describes how they move from one group to the other. **Fitzgerald deliberately holds the narrator's attraction to and disgust with the party in tight tension throughout the extract**;[8] in doing so, he powerfully highlights the beauty of the event amidst the **swirl of 'gaudy' and lurching guests**.[9]

The cover art to the first edition of The Great Gatsby.

A Special Event

SECTION B: CREATIVE WRITING

Question Five: Guidance

Now, I'm no creative writer, and this question can be daunting for students. But I want to suggest a way around them. To begin with, practice makes perfect and whilst you might not have time to write out each response, you can at least plan a series of responses to various generic prompts. Just engaging your imagination in this way can be a really useful exercise.

The marks for Question Five are split into two: AO5 (Content and Organisation) and AO6 (Technical Accuracy).

The terms of AO5 can be split and independently defined: 'Content' refers to your register (that is, the tone and vocabulary you use to grab your audience) and the way in which your piece is matched to its purpose (hence those little pre-ambles about entering an online or newspaper competition) — but also the ideas and techniques you employ in your creative writing piece. 'Organisation' meanwhile refers to your use of structure alongside ideas that are, for top marks, compelling and convincing.

AO6 is what we might reductively call Spelling, Punctuation and Grammar (SPaG), but at the top of the mark scheme it is about both accuracy and using a range of sentence structures and ambitious vocabulary. To access the top end of the scheme, there also needs to be a range of punctuation used (ideally including brackets, colons and semi-colons).

As I said in the answer to Questions Two and Three, the techniques you analyse in your English Language GCSE are the same as the English Literature GCSE. Just as you **analyse** how others use these techniques for effect (always for effect), you should (or, even, *must*) **use** these in your creative writing response. Through the three examples presented in this book, I'm going to show you some of the ways you write these techniques into your own creative writing.

You may be presented with a picture and the prompt to 'Describe' something based on the image. Carefully look at this picture: are there any details that surprise you? Try and put that picture into motion so that you can think what happens next (you might also think what has happened before). Again, practice makes perfect: take random pictures from newspapers or online articles and spend 10 minutes writing a description. With some hard work, you'll soon find that Question Five is not as bad as it seems (and if I can write four short stories, you certainly can).

As with the reading analysis I've included a commentary on the left-hand side to show you my creative process – hopefully from this you'll realise that there can be a method to writing creatively that makes the task somewhat easier. If you know your techniques well, you can write them into your work. So spend time thinking about which similes or metaphors would work in certain scenarios: what similes would you use, for example, to describe a crowded place or a cold environment?

Question Five: Exemplar

Write a story about a special event.

**(24 marks for content and organisation
16 marks for technical accuracy)
[40 marks]**

With another loud explosion[1] *the sparks spread into the air. Glimmering arms of red, green and gold announce themselves with great aplomb as an awed silence passed throughout the crowd.*

The **echoes** *of Big Ben* **chiming** *in the New Year come from the television indoors, which also shows crowds of people packed in* **like sardines**.[2] *Here the garden is littered with members of my family: my son with his partner, my other son alone, and my daughter with her* **(rather drunk)**[3] *husband.*

1) I'm beginning mid-story so that I don't have any awkward setting up. It also lets me reach a conclusion quicker without having to rush through the piece.

*2) **Appropriate words to describe Big Ben and a simple simile.** 3) **Using brackets to add extra information.** 4) **I'm using rhetorical questions to suggest the frustrated tone of my narrator.** 5) **Another simile, this time to suggest how the fireworks might be imagined negatively.** 6) **A few well-placed adjectives can really add to your piece.** 7) **I'm using speech marks to suggest the irony with which my narrator views the world (gall means bold and impudent behaviour).** 8) **A considered verb that also suggests the age of my cranky narrator.** 9) **Throughout this paragraph I'm using brackets to give a real sense of my narrator's internal voice, which is consistently moaning.** 10) **A shift in my narrative with a short sentence for effect.** 11) **A short paragraph, again to stress the changing tone.** 12) **An oxymoron.** 13) **A fun little detail in parenthesis, just to show some extra creativity.** 14) **As noted before, speech is hard, so it's good to use it here as a clue to the story.**

Why are people so obsessed with celebrating the New Year? What's so special about celebrating the unknown? **What's so exciting about another year?**[4]

As clouds of blue smoke float into the night sky, it's easy to see an ugliness: each firework lets off more sparks that look **like glittering tentacles reaching into the coming year.**[5]

Tired of the **biting**[6] *cold, I move towards the back door. That's another thing about this time of year: why does so much of it necessitate being outdoors? It starts with Halloween, that brooding evening of fancy dress, and goes on throughout what some people have the gall to call* **"the most wonderful time of the year".**[7]

I **shuffle**[8] *towards the warmth of my son's house, extending my new walking stick (a sick gift from 'Santa') with each step. There's a slight step into his new, modern kitchen. With an island of black stone, exposed lights and underfloor heating (not that I'd know, I'm wearing my trusted slippers), it's impressive, but cold. Not in terms of temperature* **(that's what the heating is for)**,[9] *but in its character; it's metallic and sterile.*

Then I see her.[10] *Slumped awkwardly in the armchair, my grand-daughter, aged five, dressed in a pink tutu with a yellow jumper. Eyes closed, chubby cheeks and her fist tightly gripping a purple crayon.*

No matter how annoyed or angry I might feel at the world, seeing her always makes me smile.[11]

She is content with some mushed banana and some quiet music. In the years to come, it's likely I too will be happy with the same things. A declarative bang outside causes her small eyes to barely open before, with a resigned sigh, she settles comfortably into what seems a **painless contortion.**[12]

Steps outside signal that the "display" has finished **(hopefully my son has not singed any of his remaining hair away)**[13] *and the drunken masses return to what had become a place of calm. Smatterings of "Wasn't that fun," "It's been so nice to see everyone again" and* **"Mum would've loved that"**[14] *can be heard.*

But as they take the small step in, what they see surprises them: their miserable father sits in his recently-deceased wife's favourite chair with

his grand-daughter firmly in his arms, their chests rising and falling in unison.[15]

15) I decided to finish the story by changing the perspective, moving out of the narrator's mind to a third-person perspective. This way, I get to reveal the slight twist (that his wife has died, hence his unpleasant behaviour) and bring it all to (what I think is) a neat and wholesome conclusion. It's not too complicated and it leaves a happy feeling in your mind.

Fireworks over Big Ben and the Palace of Westminster.

Sample Paper Two

SECTION A: EDITH WHARTON'S ETHAN FROME; SECTION B: A JOURNEY

A snowy vista in Massachusetts, USA.

Edith Wharton's Ethan Frome

SECTION A: READING

Source A: This extract is from the beginning of Edith Wharton's *Ethan Frome* (1911). In the novel, an unnamed narrator has just arrived in Starkfield for work.

1   I had been sent up by my employers on a job connected with the big power-house at
    Corbury Junction, and a long-drawn carpenters' strike had so delayed the work that I
    found myself anchored at Starkfield—the nearest habitable spot—for the best part of
    the winter. I chafed at first, and then, under the hypnotising effect of routine, gradu-
5   ally began to find a grim satisfaction in the life. During the early part of my stay I had
    been struck by the contrast between the vitality of the climate and the deadness of
    the community. Day by day, after the December snows were over, a blazing blue sky
    poured down torrents of light and air on the white landscape, which gave them back
    in an intenser glitter. One would have supposed that such an atmosphere must
10 quicken the emotions as well as the blood; but it seemed to produce no change except
    that of retarding still more the sluggish pulse of Starkfield. When I had been there a
    little longer, and had seen this phase of crystal clearness followed by long stretches of
    sunless cold; when the storms of February had pitched their white tents about the
    devoted village and the wild cavalry of March winds had charged down to their
15 support; I began to understand why Starkfield emerged from its six months' siege like
    a starved garrison capitulating without quarter. Twenty years earlier the means of
    resistance must have been far fewer, and the enemy in command of almost all the
    lines of access between the beleaguered villages; and, considering these things, I felt
    the sinister force of Harmon's phrase: "Most of the smart ones get away." But if that

20   were the case, how could any combination of obstacles have hindered the flight of a
      man like Ethan Frome?

      During my stay at Starkfield I lodged with a middle-aged widow colloquially known
      as Mrs. Ned Hale. Mrs. Hale's father had been the village lawyer of the previous
      generation, and "lawyer Varnum's house," where my landlady still lived with her
25   mother, was the most considerable mansion in the village. It stood at one end of the
      main street, its classic portico and small-paned windows looking down a flagged path
      between Norway spruces to the slim white steeple of the Congregational church. It
      was clear that the Varnum fortunes were at the ebb, but the two women did what
      they could to preserve a decent dignity; and Mrs. Hale, in particular, had a certain
30   wan refinement not out of keeping with her pale old-fashioned house.

      In the "best parlour," with its black horse-hair and mahogany weakly illuminated by a
      gurgling Carcel lamp, I listened every evening to another and more delicately shaded
      version of the Starkfield chronicle. It was not that Mrs. Ned Hale felt, or affected, any
      social superiority to the people about her; it was only that the accident of a finer
35   sensibility and a little more education had put just enough distance between herself
      and her neighbours to enable her to judge them with detachment. She was not
      unwilling to exercise this faculty, and I had great hopes of getting from her the
      missing facts of Ethan Frome's story, or rather such a key to his character as should
      co-ordinate the facts I knew. Her mind was a store-house of innocuous* anecdote and
40   any question about her acquaintances brought forth a volume of detail; but on the
      subject of Ethan Frome I found her unexpectedly reticent. There was no hint of
      disapproval in her reserve; I merely felt in her an insurmountable reluctance to speak
      of him or his affairs, a low "Yes, I knew them both... it was awful..." seeming to be
      the utmost concession that her distress could make to my curiosity.

      * Innocuous – not harmful or offensive.

      ─────────────

Question One: Guidance

This opening question worth four marks is meant to ease you into the exam. It
will usually be set on the first few lines of the source.

A small point to note about my answers is that I have used full sentences.
Students that write in full sentences are more likely to get full marks for this
question than those who just write notes.

Question One: Exemplar

Read again the first part of the source, from lines **1 to 5.**

List **four** things readers learn about the narrator from this part of the source.

[4 marks]

1. *He is living at Starkfield because it's the nearest habitable place.*
2. *He has been sent to the area by his work.*
3. *He is meant to be working at the power house.*
4. *At first he struggled but then came to enjoy his time there.*

Question Two: Guidance

If you take anything from this guide (alongside my notes and suggestions), I'd love for you to remember one thing: just like in English Literature, the texts you study for English Language have been actively constructed by the writer. By that I mean that the author of the text you're analysing – be they William Shakespeare or a contemporary novelist – one day sat down and decided to use that simile, that short sentence, that long paragraph, that… you get the idea.

The main challenge with Question Two is that you must write about **effect.** Simply listing a technique ('There is an adverb here' or 'The author includes a simile') will not gain you many marks. To get into the top band for this question (and Question Three), you must utilise, according to the mark scheme, 'detailed, perceptive analysis'. What is needed here is a consideration of how these techniques are **used** by the author. You'll see below that no technique or word is quoted without including a discussion in some form of its effect. Terminology, as previous Examiner's Reports have made clear, should only be used to enhance responses.

(You should be consulting Examiner's Reports for all your subjects – they include a wealth of tips and tricks that can really help you understand where students go right (and, perhaps more importantly, where they go wrong)).

You may also notice how in the majority of my answers I group my points into 'big idea' paragraphs. For example, in the answer below I discuss how the writer uses military language at length. This method of applying themes to each of your paragraphs will allow you to tie your points and analysis together under unifying banners, and will give your answers a more formal structure.

Also, on an issue of practicality – the exam board will provide the extract for Question Two in a box above the question. Before beginning Question Two, make sure you re-read the text and annotate it: keep the text as fresh in your mind as possible!

Question Two: Exemplar

Look in detail at this extract, from **lines 5 to 16** of the source:

During the early part of my stay I had been struck by the contrast between the vitality of the climate and the deadness of the community. Day by day, after the December snows were over, a blazing blue sky poured down torrents of light and air on the white landscape, which gave them back in an intenser glitter. One would have supposed that such an atmosphere must quicken the emotions as well as the blood; but it seemed to produce no change except that of retarding still more the sluggish pulse of Starkfield. When I had been there a little longer, and had seen this phase of crystal clearness followed by long stretches of sunless cold; when the storms of February had pitched their white tents about the devoted village and the wild cavalry of March winds had charged down to their support; I began to understand why Starkfield emerged from its six months' siege like a starved garrison capitulating without quarter.

How does the writer use language here to describe Starkfield's harsh environment?

You could include the writer's choice of:

- Words and phrases
- Language features and techniques
- Sentence forms.

[8 marks]

*At the beginning of the extract, the narrator establishes the 'contrast between the vitality of the climate and the deadness of the community.' As such, **the writer emphasizes constantly how vivid Starkfield is as a space but there is also a focus on how violent the weather is there.**[1] For example, once the snow has settled the 'blazing blue sky poured down torrents of light and air', with the writer's use of stronger verbs emphasizing how bright the environment is. The word 'torrents' adds to the strength of this light, suggesting it is almost uncontrollable. This strong light is reflected off the snow with an even 'intenser glitter': the writer's oxymoron*

1) I've now established my argument for my response, showing how I have understood the extract.

here creates an environment that is blindingly bright. Because nature is here so powerful, it is unsurprising that Starkfield is described as having a 'sluggish pulse', as if the inhabitants are being suffocated by nature's power.

2) I've integrated the quotation into my prose and then I've moved straight into the analysis. 3) In this final paragraph I've gathered all the evidence together and used it to present an argument. This thematic approach helps bring all my analysis together and makes the response feel less like a checklist of techniques. 4) When writing about sound effects, it's always good to draw attention exactly to the sound to make it clear for the marker. 5) I often suggest finishing your analysis for Question 2 with the end of the extract: it gives your work a natural tone of closure and lets you offer a final point of analysis.

The writer creates an overall impression of how Starkfield is both beautiful and harsh. The narrator talks of **phases 'of crystal clearness followed by long stretches of sunless cold'.**[2] *The word 'crystal' suggests a purity that is then followed by an almost apocalyptic existence without a hope of a break from the freezing environments.*

This darker awareness is carried into the final lines of the extract that **use military language**[3] *to imply the locals of Starkfield are waging war with the weather. With February comes 'pitched' white piles of snow (the 'tents'), suggesting how it will be there for a while, whilst in March the 'wild cavalry' of 'winds' charge to the village. Even if these winds offer some support, the personification and martial language imply the vicious nature of how the weather attacks the town, which is also emphasized by the* **alliterative 'w' sound**[4] *('wild cavalry of March winds') that adds a quickening pace to the lines.* **At the end of the extract,**[5] *then, it is unsurprising that the narrator uses a simile to describe how the town emerges from the weather's 'siege like a starved garrison'. The narrator thus shows how the harsh environment of Starkfield, for all its façade of beauty, enacts a war of attrition* on its inhabitants with deadly consequences.*

* Attrition – a prolonged period of conflict wherein both sides hope to gradually weaken the other.

Question Three: Guidance

What does AQA mean when they say 'structure'? At its simplest form, it is about how a text is **organised**. As explained in the mark scheme for Paper One, structural features can include: shifts within the source as a whole (what does the extract focus on at the beginning and how has that changed by the end?); shifts within a paragraph (how do topics change?) or the length of sentences (are they short and pithy or long and rambling?).

Some other structural features that you might want to write about include: shifts in perspective or focus; flashbacks or flashforwards; lists; levels of detail (going in and out to focus on small and larger things); repetition; circular structures (when the story begins and ends in the same place, or with a similar quotation) and foreshadowing.

Writing on effect and structure is much the same as language: you need to say what the structural feature does to the text and your reading of it. The way you do this will determine your mark: for example, in the November 2017 Examiner's Report, it was noted that tracking shifts across the text is a Level 2 (3-4 marks) skill. What matters, however, is your discussion of **why** these shifts happen and what the impact of these is on the reader.

Question Three: Exemplar

You now need to think about the **whole** of the source.

This text is near the beginning of a novel.

How has the writer structured the text to interest you as a reader?

You could write about:

- What the writer focuses your attention on at the beginning of the source.
- How and why the writer changes this focus as the source develops
- Any other structural features that interest you.

[8 marks]

*Early in the source, the narrator states he was 'struck by the contrast between the vitality of the climate and the deadness of the community.' The writer maintains this tension throughout the structure of the source with long paragraphs each **focusing on one theme: respectively, the weather, his lodgings and his conversations with Mrs Hale**.[1] These long paragraphs present the reader with extended tableaus of the narrator's life in Starkfield that encourage us to learn more about such a harsh place.*

*During the first paragraph, which describes the weather at Starkfield, the narrator **begins** by acknowledging some of the beauty to be found there. **By the end of the paragraph, however**,[2] the narrator is focusing on how defeated the inhabitants are, **suggesting how the weather has chipped away at their resolve**:[3] there is no longer any beauty to be found at this place. Within this paragraph the writer focuses on the weather in January, February and March; the prose thus becomes a record of the continuous*

*1) **I'm showing my knowledge of the text here.** 2) **I'm comparing here how the focus of a single paragraph changes; notice the comparative language ('however') and the notes that guide my reader through my answer (such as 'begins' and 'By the end')... 3)...but I'm also linking this shift to an effect (this skill is what brings my work into the higher marks).***

suffering experienced there. Hence the question that ends the paragraph (about why Ethan Frome has not yet left Starkfield) has an understandable resonance, and the reader too wants to find out more about this mysterious figure.

4) Again I'm summarizing the text and noticing how our interest is manipulated during the work. 5) A quick quotation to support my point. 6) Again I've taken my response right to the end of the extract so that I cannot be accused of not engaging with the text in its entirety in some form.

This desire to learn more about Ethan Frome is delayed however **because the second paragraph describes the Hales' house.**[4] *The house is disappointing both in terms of its condition (the narrator observes how the* **'Varnum fortunes were at the ebb')**[5] *and because it delays the narrative, meaning the question posed at the end of the first paragraph continues to be unanswered. Even when the narrator speaks with Mrs Hale, he finds her 'unexpectedly reticent' to speak about Frome; the writer thus constantly delays our finding out about Frome,* **meaning the reader shares the narrator's 'curiosity' constantly.**[6]

Question Four: Guidance

It has been noted in Examiner's Reports that the more able students often begin with their own evaluation and then build an argument that supports this. It is essential, therefore, that you **plan** your response, even if briefly.

The first thing you should do, however, before you begin to plan is to **re-read the chosen lines** with a focus on the question. It might seem repetitive but to not do so means you might miss out on certain bits.

Question Four: Exemplar

Focus this part of your answer on the second part of the source, from line 22 to the end.

Upon reading this extract, a student said, 'Even though the Hale house is described as a "mansion", the writer shows how disappointing the place and its inhabitants are.'

To what extent do you agree?

In your response, you could:

- Evaluate how the writer depicts the house.
- Consider how Mrs Hale is presented.
- Support your response with references to the text.

[20 marks]

*1) **Continuing analysis to show how a writer creates meaning.** 2) **Using the terms of the question at the end of each paragraph shows how the response is convincing and critical.** 3) **My quotations are integrated into my prose and constantly analytical in tone.** Broadly I try not to quote without offering some point of analysis. 4) **A quick quotation just to support my interpretation.** 5) **The occasional adjective can be useful to signal your interpretation and understanding of the passage.** 6) **I refer to previous paragraphs of analysis so that my response cumulatively builds as I continue working through the passage.***

*The Hales's home is described as a 'considerable mansion', with features like a 'classic portico' and its pretty view suggesting how it was once a fine place to live. But, as suggested by the student, Wharton deflates these seemingly grandiose traits throughout the extract. In noting how 'the Varnum fortunes were at the ebb', the writer stresses how their wealth, just like the tide, is slowly being drawn out. Nonetheless, Mrs Hale and her mother do try to 'preserve a decent dignity', with the **strong alliterative 'd' sound implying their determination.**[1] Yet the word 'preserve' also suggests how this task is doomed to fail, for whilst they may be able to keep the house in some state, it will eventually fully decompose. **It is unsurprising, really, that the narrator is a little disappointed in such a 'pale old-fashioned house.'**[2]*

*As Wharton moves from an over-view of the house to a specific room, she uses quotation marks to add some irony to the idea that the narrator is now in the 'best parlour'. In this room, there is a 'gurgling' lamp, which shows how the lamp is barely working, and possibly adding an unnatural, hollow noise that weakly fills the darkened room. **The narrator titles Mrs Hale as the 'Starkfield chronicle', a wry reference to her gossiping nature. The word 'chronicle' implies she knows everything about the villagers, which is also highlighted in the description of her 'store-house of innocuous anecdote[s]'.**[3] The 'store-house' metaphor suggests Mrs Hale's compendium of knowledge; the stories she tells are not **harmful ('innocuous')**[4] but at the same time her passive nature seems to bore the narrator. Mrs Hale is noted as having a 'certain wan refinement not out of keeping with her pale' house: the word 'wan' suggests pale weakness and, just like the house, Mrs Hale does not entice the narrator.*

*This disappointment continues when the narrator asks about Ethan Frome, a person he does want to learn about. Whereas Mrs Hale has a long list of stories to tell about all the other villagers, on Frome she is decidedly quiet. Aside from the brevity of her utterance, Wharton **teasingly**[5] uses ellipses to suggest how there is a much larger story to be told: 'Yes, I knew them both…' she explains, 'it was awful…' Where the stories about everyone else were 'innocuous', this story is evidently full of meaning and sadness. **Her decision not to share this, then, in such a drab and dark place, overall**[6] paints an image of a cold, disappointing house in which to spend any amount of time would be a challenge.*

The narrator also touches on the Hales's own separation from the rest of the town. Mrs Hale is said to have had 'a finer sensibility and a little more education' than the rest of the village. This distance implies how lonely the family might be. **In a place named 'Starkfield'**[7] such isolation is all the more cutting. **Together,**[8] the encroaching dilapidation of the house, and the selectively mystic but separate Mrs Hall imply the quiet, unexpressive and **disappointing** tone that occupies the entirety of the passage – **stark indeed**.[9]

7) Don't forget to think about the names of places and characters. As here, they can be telling. 8) I'm reminding the examiner of everything I've discussed in the response. 9) A little rhetorical flourish to finish my response, but note how I've used the key term from the question so it's clear the response is focused.

Early cover art for Edith Wharton's Ethan Frome

A Journey

SECTION B: CREATIVE WRITING

Question Five: Guidance

A note on planning – examiner's reports from previous years of this exam have stressed the importance of planning. It has been noted in these reports how students can struggle because they have not spent sufficient time planning. You are to spend roughly 45 minutes on this question. It would be wise to spend five minutes planning and another five editing at the end of your work. Planning can help you avoid writing too much (quality is preferred over quantity in this question); it can help you think through your ideas, which is especially useful if you want to include a twist at the end of your work; and it's an opportunity to breathe and think before launching in (it's best to have ideas that are formed in your mind before you start writing). That said, do not spend too much time planning: you need to actually give yourself enough time to write! In the response below, I've added a few minor details towards the end to give my story a slight twist. Careful planning helped me realise where was best to add these details.

This is where practice makes perfect. If you're unsure how to use certain pieces of punctuation, research them and write some sample sentences. I also suggest you make a glossary of words that have more impressive synonyms (so using 'scalding' instead of 'hot', or 'mischievous' instead of 'naughty') so that when you're writing you are not thinking of the best alternatives. If you use basic vocabulary, no matter how accurate it is, you may struggle to get beyond Level 2 (5-8 marks). You might want to also think about other techniques – such as similes and oxymorons – that can be used in certain scenarios (and for effect, of course).

The main thing is that to access the top band for AO5, that is Level 4 (19-24 marks), your writing needs to be 'compelling' and 'convincing'. To achieve this, working on your written expression and ideas will ensure each sentence, each word choice and each technique is matched to purpose in a way that keeps your marker reading on. It's a challenge, certainly, but one well worth accepting!

Finally, and I cannot stress this enough, you should be reading widely as you study for your GCSEs. If you don't know what to read, go into your local bookstore and ask for their recommendations. Students that struggle with creative writing often don't read in their spare time, and it can often show: just losing yourself in a good book every once in a while will really help spark your imagination. In much the same way, you should try to enjoy this opportunity to creatively express yourself!

Write a story with the title 'a journey'.

(24 marks for content and organisation
16 marks for technical accuracy)
[40 marks]

As I rush to catch the elevator,[1] *I barely notice the man in **b**lack standing at the **b**ack of the **b**oxed space.[2] After catching my breath, the doors of the elevator close. I turn and look at his gaunt, sombre face with an apologetic smile across my own.*

Nothing.[3]

No *recognition,* ***no*** *"hello" or "welcome",* ***no***[4] *desire to talk with me about the day ahead or even the weather. Instead he just stands there, still as a statue.*

It is, you might say, typical London behaviour;[5] a world of isolated egotism.

Amidst my internal rant about the state of the world, the realisation that I am in an unfamiliar environment slowly begins to dawn on me. For years I've taken the same journey:[6] a five-minute walk from my two-bedroom flat, followed by a forty-minute trip on the tube and a quick two-minute flight in the same elevator that trudges my colleagues and I to our daily grind.

*1) **I begin the story** in **medias res**, or 'in the middle of things', as a way of getting the reader hooked. 2) **Notice my use of alliteration** (the repeated 'b' sound). 3) **Use a variety of paragraph lengths for effect.** 4) **The repetition of 'no'** is to add emphasis to the narrator's exasperated tone. 5) **Using a varied selection of punctuation is a key part of the AO6 mark scheme.** 6) **Here I'm using a colon to introduce a list,** showing as wide a range of punctuation as possible.*

But today, something is different. Everything looks bright — **perhaps the caretaker of the building finally fixed the second light in the lift?**[7] *I take off my glasses and notice a long crack in the left lens.*

Before I can process this unusual occurrence and press the button for the fifteenth floor, that hellish space in which I have poured so many years of my life for no real purpose, the stranger steps forward silently, presses the button for his own destination and the doors close.[8]

Suddenly, the elevator **shudders**[9] *into life and begins a slow ascent. Again, as if nothing happened, we stand in silence. But I notice how the walls of this small box feel as if they are contracting. A small bead of sweat begins to creep down my spine* **(prompting an involuntary shiver)**[10] *and I try to loosen the collar of my shirt.*

Only then do I realise the red mark on my clothing. A bloom of scarlet has stained my arm. How frustrating: this was a new shirt! As I slowly trace these blotches up my arm, I realise the soft fabric is also torn and dirty.[11]

I can't remember how I got here. **The last thing I remember was a flash of lights before—**[12]

Just as the **glimmer**[13] *of recognition slips into my mind, I notice how the anonymous stranger who has stood by me for all this time has slowly, almost imperceptibly, begun to move again.*

His hand, which is enveloped with a thin layer of skin, **scuttles**[14] *onto my shoulder.*

"This," he says, "is where you get off."[15]

A non-threatening ding announces our arrival and as the doors open I realise my destination. It's beaut—[16]

7) Humour can add real character to your work; failing that, rhetorical questions can help suggest a desire to understand what is happening. 8) Be cautious about having over-long sentences (they risk rambling and your grammar can get lost) but you must also have a variety of sentence lengths. 9) 'Shudders' gives a sense of fear or discomfort, which is matched by the narrator. 10) Brackets (or parenthesis) can be a great way of adding extra detail; here it's as if the line itself has an 'involuntary shiver' through the addition. 11) I keep trying to use sentences of varying lengths to keep an uncomfortable, searching pace to the work. 12) At this point I feel it is good to get the narrative moving towards an end point. 13) 'Glimmer' has something slightly undefinable to it. 14) 'Scuttles' has an uncomfortable feel to it. 15) Writing dialogue is difficult, and should be used sparingly (a response that is introspective and reflective will, largely, be more engaging than something action packed and with excessive dialogue). 16) Endings are always difficult, and here I have decided not to state what the character sees but instead leave the reader teetering on the edge of understanding.

Sample Paper Three

SECTION A: VIRGINIA WOOLF'S KEW GARDENS; SECTION B: AUTUMNAL DESCRIPTION

A dragonfly in action.

Virginia Woolf's Kew Gardens

Source A: This extract is from the beginning of Virginia Woolf's short story 'Kew Gardens' (1919) in which short snippets of the lives of four couples passing the flowerbeds are explored.

1 From the oval-shaped flower-bed there rose perhaps a hundred stalks spreading into heart-shaped or tongue-shaped leaves half way up and unfurling at the tip red or blue or yellow petals marked with spots of colour raised upon the surface; and from the red, blue or yellow gloom of the throat emerged a straight bar, rough with gold dust
5 and slightly clubbed at the end. The petals were voluminous* enough to be stirred by the summer breeze, and when they moved, the red, blue and yellow lights passed one over the other, staining an inch of the brown earth beneath with a spot of the most intricate colour. The light fell either upon the smooth, grey back of a pebble, or, the shell of a snail with its brown, circular veins, or falling into a raindrop, it expanded
10 with such intensity of red, blue and yellow the thin walls of water that one expected them to burst and disappear. Instead, the drop was left in a second silver grey once more, and the light now settled upon the flesh of a leaf, revealing the branching thread of fibre beneath the surface, and again it moved on and spread its illumination in the vast green spaces beneath the dome of the heart-shaped and tongue-shaped
15 leaves. Then the breeze stirred rather more briskly overhead and the colour was flashed into the air above, into the eyes of the men and women who walk in Kew Gardens in July.

The figures of these men and women straggled past the flower-bed with a curiously

20   irregular movement not unlike that of the white and blue butterflies who crossed the turf in zig-zag flights from bed to bed. The man was about six inches in front of the woman, strolling carelessly, while she bore on with greater purpose, only turning her head now and then to see that the children were not too far behind. The man kept this distance in front of the woman purposely, though perhaps unconsciously, for he wished to go on with his thoughts.

25   "Fifteen years ago I came here with Lily," he thought. "We sat somewhere over there by a lake and I begged her to marry me all through the hot afternoon. How the dragonfly kept circling round us: how clearly I see the dragonfly and her shoe with the square silver buckle at the toe. All the time I spoke I saw her shoe and when it moved impatiently I knew without looking up what she was going to say: the whole of her

30   seemed to be in her shoe. And my love, my desire, were in the dragonfly; for some reason I thought that if it settled there, on that leaf, the broad one with the red flower in the middle of it, if the dragonfly settled on the leaf she would say "Yes" at once. But the dragonfly went round and round: it never settled anywhere—of course not, happily not, or I shouldn't be walking here with Eleanor and the children—Tell me,

35   Eleanor. D'you ever think of the past?"

"Why do you ask, Simon?"

"Because I've been thinking of the past. I've been thinking of Lily, the woman I might have married.... Well, why are you silent? Do you mind my thinking of the past?"

"Why should I mind, Simon? Doesn't one always think of the past, in a garden with
40   men and women lying under the trees? Aren't they one's past, all that remains of it, those men and women, those ghosts lying under the trees, ... one's happiness, one's reality?"

* Voluminous – large and open.

Question One: Guidance

Not all students receive full marks for this question, often either because they have read the wrong section (notice the question says 'from this part of the source') or they misinterpret the source.

Question One: Exemplar

Read again the first part of the source, from lines **1 to 5.**

List **four** things readers learn about the flower bed from this part of the source.

[4 marks]

1. *There are a lot of flowers, 'perhaps a hundred'.*
2. *The flowers are red, yellow and blue in colour.*
3. *The flower bed is oval shaped.*
4. *The flowers have opened (the 'straight bar').*

Question Two: Guidance

Students often struggle because they label features incorrectly (worse still, they 'device spot' – meaning, you name a technique and move on without discussing its effect (by now you should know that's not what you do)), examine word connotations without an awareness of textual context (e.g. saying the colour red represents anger in any text) or they select lengthy quotations from the text. On that last point: short, integrated quotations in your own prose is the best way of quoting from the text. Otherwise your answer becomes more a paraphrase of the source, not an analysis. Remember, we want to hear your analysis of the text, not just a regurgitation of the source!

Question Two: Exemplar

Look in detail at this extract, from **lines 5 to 17** of the source:

The petals were voluminous enough to be stirred by the summer breeze, and when they moved, the red, blue and yellow lights passed one over the other, staining an inch of the brown earth beneath with a spot of the most intricate colour. The light fell either upon the smooth, grey back of a pebble, or, the shell of a snail with its brown, circular veins, or falling into a raindrop, it expanded with such intensity of red, blue and yellow the thin walls of water that one expected them to burst and disappear. Instead, the drop was left in a second silver grey once more, and the light now settled upon the flesh of a leaf, revealing the branching thread of fibre beneath the surface, and again it moved on and spread its illumination in the vast green spaces beneath the dome of the heart-shaped and tongue-shaped leaves. Then the breeze stirred rather more briskly overhead and the colour was flashed into the air above, into the eyes of the men and women who walk in Kew Gardens in July.

How does the writer use language here to describe the flower bed?

You could include the writer's choice of:

- Words and phrases
- Language features and techniques
- Sentence forms.

[8 marks]

1) I'm here using brackets just to explain my thinking. 2) Here I show how I'm sensitive to various meanings of individual words. 3) Through my quotations, I'm ranging throughout the text. 4) It's fine to briefly refer outside of the extract just to provide extra evidence for your point. But notice how I tie it back to the text at the end of my answer.

From the beginning of the extract, the writer balances the rich 'voluminous' flowers with a tone of gentleness. The flowers are 'stirred by the summer breeze', which implies their soft movement as suggested by both the word 'stirred' **(which is a gentle verb)**[1] *and 'breeze' (which suggests how the wind is lightly moving the flowers; the writer does not say 'wind', for example). Amidst this environment, when the light from the flowers is described as 'staining' the earth,* **it is not done so within a negative frame; quite the opposite, in fact,**[2] *for against the dull 'brown earth' the bright yellows, blues and reds of the flowers have an enlivening power.*

Woolf uses repetition in noting the colours of the flowers throughout the extract, and contrasts this against the brown earth, the 'silver grey' of the water droplet and the 'vast green' stems of the flowers. The writer thus uses colour to suggest how vibrant these flowers are and how they stand out in their environment.[3]

Alongside the focus on the colour of the flowers, the writer uses language related to the human body to suggest how nature is here alive. The leaves of the flowers are not only repetitively described as 'heart-shaped and tongue-shaped' but they also are noted as having 'flesh'. **Just before the provided extract, the flowers are also noted as having a 'throat'.**[4] *This personification of the leaves, along with the focus on the colour of the garden patch, shows how this flowerbed is alive and pretty.*

Question Three: Guidance

Students can lose marks in Question Three by just explaining what happens in the text (remember my point on AO2 earlier? If not, see pp. 5) or not explaining the effect of the technique. You have to think of *why* something is where it is in the text. You also have to write about the source in its entirety (the question highlights you must focus on 'the whole of the source).

Some students only offer general comments such as 'this interests the reader' or 'this makes the reader want to read on'. However, in showing no awareness of how structural techniques specifically effect our reading, these sorts of responses will achieve no more than 2 marks.

Question Three: Exemplar

You now need to think about the **whole** of the source.

This text is near the beginning of a novel.

How has the writer structured the text to interest you as a reader?

You could write about:

- What the writer focuses your attention on at the beginning of the source.
- How and why the writer changes this focus as the source develops
- Any other structural features that interest you.

[8 marks]

1) I'm showing an awareness of the entire paragraph first... 2) ... before analysing a single sentence. (Dappled light is that spotted light that you see when sitting under a tree). 3) Try to be attuned to repetitions within a passage, especially if at the beginning and end. 4) I'm talking about how the story moves forward.

At the beginning of the extract Woolf offers an overview of the flowerbed ('a hundred stalks') **before honing in[1]** *on the individual anatomy of individual flowers (which is emphasized by the use of references to the human body to describe the flowers). The focus on individual flowers, describing their structure, colour and design, allows readers to appreciate how beautiful and perfect each piece is. Within this opening paragraph, Woolf also examines how the dappled light from the flowers fall on pebbles, snails and then 'into a raindrop', with* **the movement from literal to metaphorical within one sentence[2]** *suggesting how the light infects everything.*

The opening paragraph of the short story **is bracketed with descriptions of the 'heart-shaped and tongue-shaped leaves'[3]** *and throughout there is a constant reminder of the blue, red and yellow colours of the flowers, suggesting the fertility of the garden bed. Yet,* **to note the narrative is moving on, Woolf changes[4]** *the reference to the light suggestion that the flowerbed was 'stirred by the summer breeze' earlier in the extract to the suggestion that 'the breeze stirred rather more briskly': the changing adverbs note the movement of the flowers and the passage then moves on to describe 'the eyes of the men and women who walk in Kew Gardens in July'.*

Of these, Woolf focuses on Simon's individual thoughts: deep in reminiscences, he is thinking of the time he was at Kew Gardens and asking Lily to marry him. As he thinks, he returns to the dragonfly that 'kept circling round us'; likewise the insect appears throughout his thoughts and exerts its hovering presence. Where Simon records his nervousness at asking Lily to marry him, Woolf uses a long sentence to suggest both his desperation: **it is as if he wants to prolong the moment in the hope that, in his memory, Lily will give a different answer.**[5]

5) To prepare for these questions, think about the various meanings sentence length (long and short) might have and then include one that is appropriate in your answer.

Question Four: Guidance

Students in the past have struggled with this question because they have speculated about the text, meaning they have written about it without any evidence. Instead this question wants you to interpret the text. Another issue that does come up is students going outside the prescribed lines too much (you can do this briefly if it helps your point, but you have been asked to focus on a certain part of the text for a reason).

Also, timing can be an issue for students here: some students spend too long on Questions Two and Three and then leave not enough time for Question Four. But Question Four is worth Questions One, Two and Three combined! As such, you need to spend time working on it properly — I would suggest somewhere in the region of 20 minutes.

Question Four: Exemplar

Focus this part of your answer on the second part of the source, **from line 25 to the end**. One student observed 'Visiting gardens always feels boring and this is no exception: nothing happens in this story.' To what extent do you agree?

In your response, you could:

- Evaluate how the writer depicts the garden.
- Consider the presentation of Simon.
- Support your response with references to the text.

[20 marks]

1) If you do disagree with the quoted opinion, say so! As long as your ideas are supported, it will produce a strong response (that said, don't disagree for the sake of it). 2) Here I'm using textual details to show my understanding of the work.

Though not a lot happens in the extract, there is a wealth of emotion and experience that can be unpicked from Woolf's short story. **To suggest, then, that this extract is 'boring' misses the point of the writer's work.**[1] To begin with, it is not uncommon to go to a place and be stimulated by memories. Once Simon begins thinking about his previous trip with Lily to Kew Gardens, it is clear how he still has feelings for her: **though he came 'fifteen years ago', the details of his memory – such as the hovering dragonfly or her 'impatient' shoe movements – suggest how he has often relived these events.**[2] To this we might add the sense of desperation when he notes how he 'begged her to marry me all through the hot afternoon.' Simon's desperation then is **presented by Woolf as something to sympathise with, not to mock or skip over.**[3]

With the dragonfly in particular, Simon attaches such importance to this small insect that it is difficult not to feel moved by his description. Instead of focusing on Lily's face or body, which would perhaps be a cliché, Woolf writes of how Simon uses the dragonfly to imagine a situation where Lily says yes; after all, he says 'my love, my desire, were in the dragonfly'. There is a hesitancy in the extract to face the truth, and in this Simon is made to be a relatable character. **The entire tone of the passage is one of contemplation,**[4] prompted by the evocative flowerbed described early on. Amidst this, there is a pain when Simon says to Eleanor 'I've been thinking of Lily, the woman I might have married', with the **ellipses**[5] that follows implying a solemn pause before he moves on. To be alert to the tone of the passage then means to find it alive with such sadness and loss. The focus on Simon's internal thoughts and memories then more than makes up for the lack of narrative action.

3) I just return to the question topic at the end but note also how I use the author's name to show her intent. 4) Writing on the author's tone is a challenge, but to do so shows you're aware of the text in an informed way. 5) I'm always trying to slip in some extra analysis. 6) My quotation is integrated with the grammar of my own writing. 7) Striking the right tone in your final line can be tough, and you don't want to appear haughty, but if your ideas have been supported and your style has been analytical, this sort of flourish may leave a lasting impression on the examiner's mind.

It is very easy, then, to agree with Eleanor when she comments 'one always thinks of the past, in a garden'. Against the living, breathing power of the flowers, Eleanor speaks of the 'ghosts lying under the trees' that are conjured when one thinks about the past. Woolf's metaphor explores how touching and emotional memories can be, and **such a somber tone inflects 'one's happiness, one's reality'.**[6] Eleanor's rhetorical questions indicate how Woolf is also asking the reader these questions. This invitation to inwardly reflect on your life then shows the strength and gentle beauty of this story – **perhaps that student should read it again**.[7]

The Royal Botanic Garden at Kew, London.

Autumnal
Description

SECTION B: CREATIVE WRITING

Question Five: Guidance

As noted in the first example answer to Question Five, students can really struggle with this task. Reports have suggested that students struggle with this question because they rely too heavily on actions and dialogue (quiet, introspective pieces allow more opportunity for description). Other issues can include mis-using vocabulary that is overly ambitious, writing too much (often due to a lack of planning) and generically re-writing the source.

Students that write pages and pages of material struggle with this question because over that sustained period the accuracy of their writing (in terms of spelling, punctuation and grammar) dips, meaning they lose marks for AO6 (being able to maintain the accuracy of your work is what distinguished Level 3 responses (which are 'mostly' accurate) from Level 2 ones (which are 'sometimes' accurate)).

The simple fact is that Question Five can be really tricky for those students who do not flex their imaginative muscles often. Keep it simple and give your story some form of narrative (meaning, give it some story so that it has a drive) that can be tied up easily and quickly if you're running out of time.

Describe a natural environment as suggested by this picture:

A colour version of this Autumnal photo can be found on this edition's cover.

**(24 marks for content and organisation
16 marks for technical accuracy)
[40 marks]**

Calm.

Calm everywhere.[1]

*As the boy steps through the forest, it is he who breaks the peaceful tranquillity of the space. The **crunch** of twigs that are **crushed** underfoot and the **puff** of frozen smoke with each sigh **violates** the landscape.*[2]

*The towering, **ancient**[3] trees exude an atmosphere of peace. A light breeze bristles their crowns of gold, causing a few more leaves to fall to the ground: another subject lost to the inevitable passing of time.*

*But at the base of these giants, there lies the beginnings of **a green rebellion**.[4] Fingers of new life grope up the wizened*

*1) **I'm opening with two incredibly short paragraphs just to give the sense of calm that's in the woods. 2) Slightly aggressive vocabulary suggests his transgression. 3) I've used 'ancient' instead of 'old', an example of where spending some time researching synonyms can be useful.***

bark **as if scaling a mountain**.[5] *Refusing to be subsumed within fields of red, orange and amber, these shoots of new life slowly creep around the forest looking for a way in.*

The trees, secure in themselves, never look down. Just as they ignore the boy trudging through their domain, so too do they not realise that something both wonderful and dangerous is coming to take over. Their arms, brittle in the decreasing temperature, stand to attention whilst the leaves can only lie and watch from a distance as the place once called home is infested.[6]

Every year, the same changes happen, yet these trees do not falter or panic. They know how to weather this storm. They tirelessly stand with the knowledge that, as always, with time their right to rule will be asserted.

*This is **not a war of artillery fire, of trenches and mortars or soldiers dying in their thousands**.[7] This is a world in which death signals new life. Reborn in **clouds of red, orange and amber**, these trees rise **like a phoenix from the flames**.[8]*

All plants look at the sun, that giver of life and air. Soon it will be dark, a perfect time for the rebels to strike and gain acres of ground. But with the sun goes their energy;[9] as evening falls they will huddle away from the cold.

Each moment, then, is vital. It is a war in which, like all wars, life awaits the winner and death the losers.[10]

But all of this is lost on the boy with the blue jacket.[11] *He walks with neglectful intent,[12] some moments bored and others awed by the magical giants who surround him. He imagines saving a princess from the goblin king who has made this his lair before soon mischievously thinking of which direction he should run away from his parents.*

*His parents watch his mindless trudging through the **sea of leaves that snap and slosh at his ankles**[13] as he charges on.*

They remark how quiet it is. How beautiful, how peaceful, how serene, they think.

Amidst the calm, there is war that rages just as it did the year before and as it will for years to come.[14]

4) ***I was struck by the green in the picture, and so am really focusing in on it to give my story some narrative.*** *5) There's nothing spectacular about my simile here, but it works, and that's what is key. 6)* ***Throughout this paragraph I'm using various sentence lengths.*** *7)* ***I'm briefly adding some details just to show some creativity.*** *8)* ***Another generic simile that is nonetheless effective because I'm emphasizing the colours of the leaves.*** *9)* ***I'm using a semi-colon here: the two sentences are linked in topic and it looks a little better than using 'and' or 'but'.*** *10)* ***A visibly shorter paragraph.*** *11)* ***A slight change in focus, now, again to add something different and help me move towards a contemplative ending.*** *12)* ***An oxymoron to inject some complexity.*** *13)* ***A simple metaphor with specific vocabulary (and a bit of alliteration, for good measure) to support it.*** *14)* ***I'm returning at the end of the piece just to the idea of the 'war' because it's my specific interpretation of the picture that is slightly different. I quietly finish without any dialogue or typical 'action'.***

Sample Paper Four

A) G. K. CHESTERTON'S THE TREMENDOUS ADVENTURES OF MAJOR BROWN; B) "I COULDN'T BELIEVE MY EYES."

Note: For the past three sample papers, I have annotated my responses so you can see how my answers correspond to the Assessment Objectives that are used to mark your answers. I've included a final sample set of answers below, and now it's time for you to annotate them yourself. Revise what each assessment objective is looking for, and then be alert to how each question is answered.

You might notice that throughout my answers in this sample paper I refer to 'the writer', not the name of the author. This is fine – in the panic of the exam you might forget the author's name – as the main point is that you're leading with an awareness that literature is actively written.

G. K. Chesterton's The Tremendous Adventures of Major Brown

SECTION A: READING

Source A: The extract is from G. K. Chesterton's short story collection 'The Club of Queer Trades' (1905). We are here introduced to the figure Major Brown.

1   One certain bright and windy afternoon, the Major, attired in his usual faultless manner, had set out for his usual constitutional. In crossing from one great residential thoroughfare to another, he happened to pass along one of those aimless-looking lanes which lie along the back-garden walls of a row of mansions, and which in their
5   empty and discoloured appearance give one an odd sensation as of being behind the scenes of a theatre. But mean and sulky as the scene might be in the eyes of most of us, it was not altogether so in the Major's, for along the coarse gravel footway was coming a thing which was to him what the passing of a religious procession is to a devout person. A large, heavy man, with fish-blue eyes and a ring of irradiating red
10   beard, was pushing before him a barrow, which was ablaze with incomparable flowers. There were splendid flowers of almost every order, but the Major's own favourite pansies predominated. The Major stopped and fell into conversation, and then into bargaining. He treated the man after the manner of collectors and other mad men, that is to say, he carefully and with a sort of anguish selected the best roots from the
15   less excellent, praised some, disparaged others, made a subtle scale ranging from a thrilling worth and rarity to a degraded insignificance, and then bought them all. the man was just pushing off his barrow when he stopped and came close to the Major.

"I'll tell you what, sir," he said. "If you're interested in them things, you just get on to that wall."

20 "On the wall!" cried the scandalized Major, whose conventional soul quailed within
him at the thought of such fantastic trespass.

"Finest show of yellow pansies in England in that there garden, sir," hissed the
tempter. "I'll help you up, sir."

How it happened no one will ever know but that positive enthusiasm of the Major's
25 life triumphed over all its negative traditions, and with an easy leap and swing that
showed that he was in no need of physical assistance, he stood on the wall at the end
of the strange garden. The second after, the flapping of the frock-coat at his knees
made him feel inexpressibly a fool. But the next instant all such trifling sentiments
were swallowed up by the most appalling shock of surprise the old soldier had ever
30 felt in all his bold and wandering existence. His eyes fell upon the garden, and there
across the large bed in the centre of the lawn was a vast pattern of pansies; they were
splendid flowers, but for once it was not their horticultural aspects that Major Brown
beheld, for the pansies were arrange in gigantic capital letters so as to the form the
sentence:

35 DEATH TO MAJOR BROWN

A kindly looking old man, with white whiskers, was watering them. Brown looked
sharply back at the road behind him; the man with the barrow had suddenly
vanished. Then he looked again at the lawn with its incredible inscription. Another
man might have thought he had gone mad, but Brown did not. When romantic ladies
40 gushed over his V.C. and his military exploits, he sometimes felt himself to be a
painfully prosaic* person, but by the same token he knew he was incurably sane.
Another man, again, might have thought himself a victim of a passing practical joke,
but Brown could not easily believe this. He knew from his own quaint learning that
the garden arrangement was an elaborate and expensive one; he thought it extrava-
45 gantly improbably that any one would pour out money like water for a joke against
him. Having no explanation whatever to offer, he admitted the fact to himself, like a
clear-headed man, and waited as he would have done in the presence of a man with
six legs.

* prosaic – lacking in imagination

Question 1: Exemplar

Read again the first part of the source, from **lines 1 to 6**.

List four things about the Major and his environment from this part of the source.

[4 marks]

1. *It is a 'bright and windy afternoon.'*
2. *The Major is out for a walk.*
3. *He is walking through a residential street.*
4. *He is currently walking down an 'aimless-looking' lane.*

Question 2: Exemplar

Look in detail at this extract, from **lines 6 to 12 of the source**.

But mean and sulky as the scene might be in the eyes of most of us, it was not altogether so in the Major's, for along the coarse gravel footway was coming a thing which was to him what the passing of a religious procession is to a devout person. A large, heavy man, with fish-blue eyes and a ring of irradiating red beard, was pushing before him a barrow, which was ablaze with incomparable flowers. There were splendid flowers of almost every order, but the Major's own favourite pansies predominated.

How does the writer use language here to describe the man?

You could include the writer's choice of:

- words and phrases
- language features and techniques
- sentence forms.

[8 marks]

The writer uses language throughout the extract to suggest both the man's odd appearance and his importance to the Major. As the man appears in the story, his importance to the Major is likened to 'a religious procession' – the writer's comparison thus shows the Major's devotional importance to the man approaching him. Yet, in spite of this significance, the man is unflatteringly referred to as a 'thing', implying his unusual appearance. Hence the scheme of reference used to describe the man – his 'fish-blue eyes' and 'irradiating red beard' – stresses his rather uncanny characteristics.

The writer is also playing with our expectations: a 'large' and 'heavy' man is the last person we might expect to be carrying a barrow full of flowers. Yet the focus on colour in his description also prepares readers for the contents of the wheelbarrow. When the writer describes how the barrow is 'ablaze with incomparable flowers', the word 'ablaze' implies the flowers are on fire, suggesting their vivid colour. This also ties to the focus on the man's 'irradiating' beard: both words suggest how the flowers and man have a way of sparking your attention and desire.

Finally, in the barrow itself the man carries 'splendid flowers of almost every order'. This outlandish claim seems at odds with the small space of the wheelbarrow. The writer thus uses language to describe a man eccentric and infectious, both outlandish and fitting to his task.

Question 3: Exemplar

You now need to think about the **whole** of the source.

This text is early on in a short story.

How has the writer structured the text to interest you as a reader?

You could write about:

- what the writer focuses your attention on at the beginning of the source.
- how and why the writer changes this focus as the source develops.
- any other structural features that interest you.

[8 marks]

At the beginning of the source, the Major's day begins as normal, a fact emphasized by the writer's repeated use of 'usual' to describe his clothing and his walk. However, by the end of the extract, the Major is in a precarious position with a flowerbed threatening his death. This transition across fifty lines keeps the reader interested, for it shows how the Major, in spite of the emphasis on his normal life, somehow gets himself into a rather awkward situation.

The longer paragraphs of the source have an ambling quality: they move through topics easily with events happening as if randomly. The writer opens a paragraph with the observation 'How it happened no one will ever know'. The first paragraph of the source describes not only the beginnings of his walk but also the man and his wheelbarrow. Throughout the passage, the long sentences together imply how the Major's attention casually moves from topic to topic. As readers, we are made to focus on these random observations, yet because of the Major's eccentricity it is curious to understand his worldview, such as his description of the backs of houses as like 'being behind the scenes of a theatre'.

The writer also uses sentence length to suggest the Major's bargaining ability. Across the long sentence, the Major praises the roots and creates a scale for the flowers, implying his knowledge and ability, only for the writer to insert the fact that he 'bought them all.' Thus the Major is made to seem both knowledgeable and foolish. The writer therefore uses structure to create a character who is an overall unusual man, his trip quickly turning into a farcical situation that can only end badly for him. Nonetheless, he is an engaging character.

Question 4: Exemplar

Focus this part of your answer on the second part of the source, from **lines 18 to the end.**

A reader, said, 'This part of the story is quite funny; the Major really has put himself in an awkward situation.'

To what extent do you agree?

In your response, you could:

- consider why the Major decides to climb the wall and what he finds there
- evaluate how the writer uses humour in the passage
- support your response with references to the text.

[20 marks]

1) Obviously I'm not suggesting you have to be aware of biblical stories (and stories from other cultures), but this is where reading widely and spending time reading about some of history's most famous stories can really help inform your analysis.

The Major is certainly an eccentric figure and the extract is indeed humorous because the writer presents him and his actions with a warm charm that somehow makes him likeable. Consequently, it's difficult not to smile as the unfolding situation slowly worsens. At the beginning of the extract, the Major is described as a 'conventional soul', with the idea of peeping over the wall described as a 'fantastic trespass'. But the writer alludes to the temptation of Adam and Eve in describing how the barrow man 'hissed' the suggestion that beyond the wall there lies a garden with the best yellow pansies in England.[1] Where Adam and Eve are tempted by the fruit of knowledge, however, the Major's interest in flowers is humorous and shows his bizarre behaviour. Such is his desire to see these flowers that he jumps up the wall with 'an easy leap and swing'; however, such physical fitness is then deflated in the next sentence with the description of his 'flapping' frock-coat: the writer therefore never allows the Major to be an outright hero, thus creating a tone of comedy throughout the passage.

Once the Major is looking in the garden the writer delays explaining the cause of 'the most appalling shock of surprise' he experiences by admitting that the flowers are indeed 'splendid'. That the message 'DEATH TO MAJOR BROWN' is described with 'gigantic' flowers adds to the bizarre situation of the story. As the Major acknowledges, the cost of such a design means they are not a joke. Yet the tone of the passage satirically ignores any real sense of threat. Added to this is 'kindly looking old man' who has 'white whiskers' – the writer's use of alliteration and focus on animalistic features ('whiskers' applies more to a cat than a human) means this gardener is a bizarre figure. Also, the sudden disappearance of the barrowman, which leaves the Major dangling from the wall, further creates a comic tone to the work. Not only is the garden unusual but also the people that surround it have an uncanny energy. The interactions of these figures with the straight-laced Major effectively creates the possibility for a strange, funny story.

The writer's use of digression in focusing on when the Major engages with 'gush[ing]' ladies about his war medals ironically acts as a counter to the suggestion that the Major is a 'prosaic person'.

Further to this, the use of similes towards the end of the passage – 'like water' and 'like a clear-headed man' – also implies the Major is slightly more poetic than he realizes. The repetition of 'Another man' implies that the Major is not as certain of his identity as he thinks, and thus the writer creates a humorous figure in a bizarre situation, from which it is impossible not to crack a smile as you read the passage.

G. K. Chesteron (the author of this extract!) in action.

"I couldn't believe my eyes."

SECTION B: CREATIVE WRITING

Question 5

Write a story that begins with the sentence: "I couldn't believe my eyes."

(24 marks for content and organisation
16 marks for technical accuracy)
[40 marks]

I couldn't believe my eyes.

Stars. Everywhere.

Growing up in London, you never see stars. The whirling mist of cloud and fog means all you ever see is the orange-tinged sky. Light pollution means nature's beauty is hidden from view. But tonight, on a school trip to a seaside town, I could see them all. Small, insignificant and proud, like flecks of paint on a blank canvas, their light radiated down and around.

Until now, it has been a boring trip. We'd come to the coast to explore the waning cliff faces and to interview local residents about their thoughts on how their town had suffered since the decline of the seaside resort. Could they remember the good times? What did they think about their town now that it was in its declining years?

"What do I think?" one person had asked. "Frankly, my dear, I don't care, as long as those immigrants don't come here."

Oblivious to the irony, they ranted for a few minutes before I managed to break away. What was most surprising about this place, however, was the sense of tiredness that lived here. At school we learnt of

*1) **I do want to point out that if you can find a way of weaving in knowledge from your other subjects, it can add a level of believability to your work. For Question 5, you might want to think about how you might include subject content from elsewhere into your creative writing piece (the same applies to the transactional writing in Paper 2).***

how seaside towns were once bustling lands of happiness and fun. Now, decimated by cheaper holidays and easier international travel, these towns have been abandoned by those who had once made so many happy memories there. All that was left was a forlorn pier and residents could only but faintly remember the former joy their town had represented for so many.

A greasy fish and chip shop fed us all. It was impressive for the staff to seem so annoyed at how much business thirty hungry children brought to the shop. Huffing and puffing as tonnes of potatoes were lowered into the bubbling oil, these people seemed resigned to a life in which nothing happened.

It was, overall, a disappointing place.

But now, as I sat on the beach and stared into the sky alone, it was also beautiful. The other students had stayed in at the hotel across the road, but I had stepped out into the fresh air. I wanted to, for a minute at least, try and understand why people would live here.

I stepped onto the beach and looked up.

Suddenly, it all made sense.

The sand, just warm from the day's sun, ran through my fingers. The waves crashed against the rocks and almost silently retreated back for safety. Somewhere below me, a worm burrowed deeper into the ground. And above me, the stars mapped infinite possibilities of life and excitement.

Little did I know that in ten years' time I would have moved to this same town. Throughout school and university, I would think back to this place; this unlikely haven. Its small houses, its small highstreet, its small people – all of it seemed perfect to me. Small and perfect. Like stars.